DUDLEY SCHOOLS LIBRARY
AND INFORMATION SERVICE

KU-798-678

Schools Library and Information Services

S00000650590

Very useful machines

Screws

Chris Oxlade

www.heinemann.co.uk/library

Visit our website to find out more information about Heinemann Library books.

To order:

☎ Phone 44 (0) 1865 888066

📄 Send a fax to 44 (0) 1865 314091

💻 Visit the Heinemann Bookshop at www.heinemann.co.uk/library to browse our catalogue and order online.

First published in Great Britain by Heinemann Library, Halley Court, Jordan Hill, Oxford OX2 8EJ, part of Harcourt Education.
Heinemann is a registered trademark of Harcourt Education Ltd.

© Harcourt Education Ltd 2003
The moral right of the proprietor has been asserted.

All rights reserved. No part of this publication may be reproduced, stored in a retrieval system, or transmitted in any form or by any means, electronic, mechanical, photocopying, recording, or otherwise, without either the prior written permission of the Publishers or a licence permitting restricted copying in the United Kingdom issued by the Copyright Licensing Agency Ltd, 90 Tottenham Court Road, London W1T 4LP (www.cla.co.uk).

Editorial: Nicole Irving and Georga Godwin
Design: Jo Hinton-Malivoire, Richard Parker and AMR
Picture Research: Rebecca Sodergren and Pete Morris
Production: Séverine Ribierre

Originated by Ambassador Litho Ltd
Printed and bound in China by South China Printing Company

ISBN 0 431 17894 1
07 06 05 04 03
10 9 8 7 6 5 4 3 2 1

British Library Cataloguing in Publication Data

Oxlade, Chris
Screws – Very Useful Machines
621.8'82
A full catalogue record for this book is available from the British Library.

Acknowledgements

The Publishers would like to thank the following for permission to reproduce photographs: Alamy Images **pp. 9**. **27**; Comstock Images/Royalty Free **pp. 23**, **25**; Corbis/Adam Woolfitt **p. 15**; Corbis/Lester Lefkowitz **p. 29**; Corbis/Robert Landau **p. 22**; Corbis/Roy Morsch **p. 11**; Corbis/Royalty-Free **p. 7**; Peter Morris **pp. 4**, **5**, **6**, **8**, **10**, **12**, **13**, **14**, **16**, **17**, **18**, **19**, **20**, **21**; SPL **p. 26**; TRIP/H Rogers **p. 24**.

Cover photograph of a screw going into a piece of wood reproduced with permission of Corbis/Royalty-Free.

Every effort has been made to contact copyright holders of any material reproduced in this book. Any omissions will be rectified in subsequent printings if notice is given to the Publishers.

Contents

DUDLEY PUBLIC LIBRARIES

L -46675

650590   SCH

J531:8

Any words appearing in the text in bold,
like this, are explained in the Glossary.

What is a screw?

screw

A machine is a man-made **device**. Machines make our lives easier by helping us to do jobs. This hook has a simple machine on the end. It is called a **screw**.

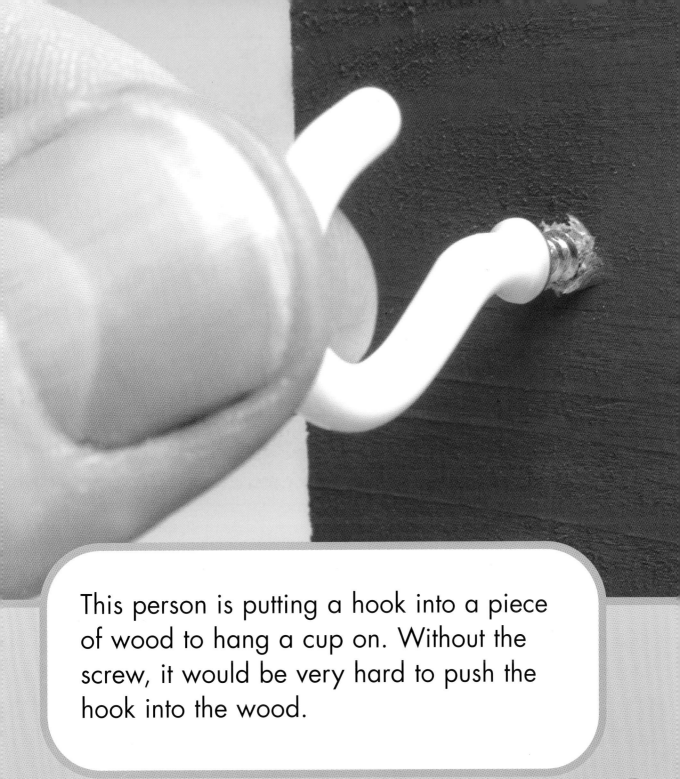

This person is putting a hook into a piece of wood to hang a cup on. Without the screw, it would be very hard to push the hook into the wood.

What does a screw do?

When a **screw** is turned, it changes a movement in one direction into movement in another direction. Turning this bottle cap makes it move up or down.

We also use screws for fixing and holding things. This light bulb has a metal screw. Turning the light bulb moves it into the holder. The screw holds the bulb in place.

How does a screw work?

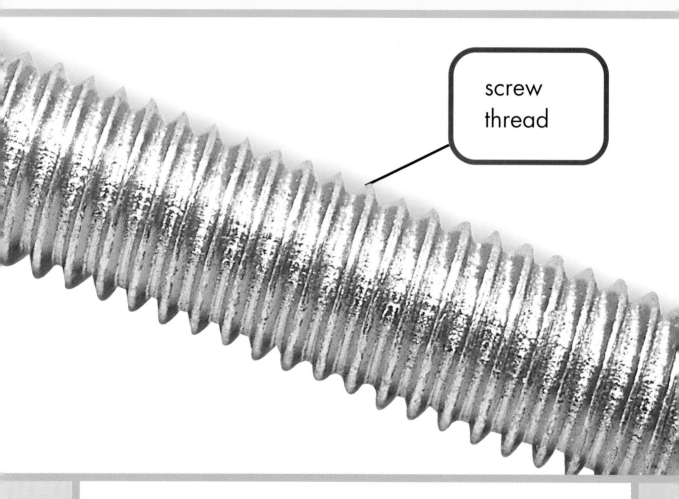

screw thread

A **screw** is made up of a piece of material with a **groove** around the outside. The groove is called a **screw thread**. Here is a close-up picture of a screw thread.

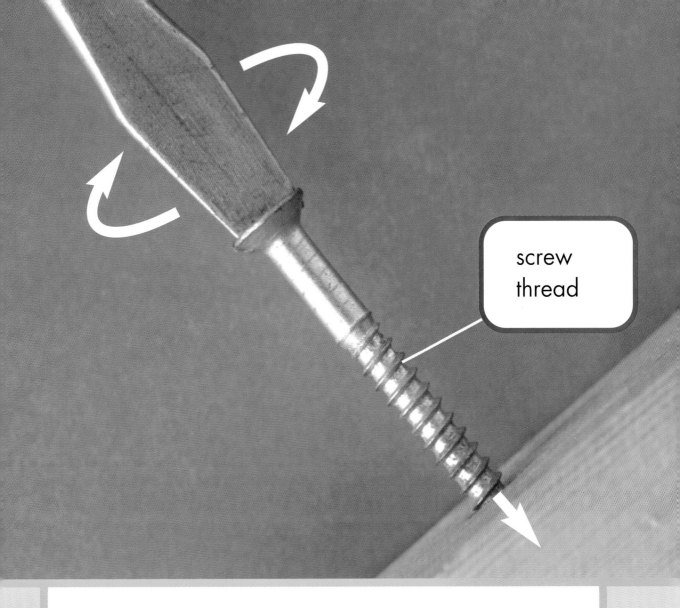

screw thread

As a screw turns, the screw thread pushes against a piece of material or against another screw thread. This makes the screw move.

Nuts and bolts

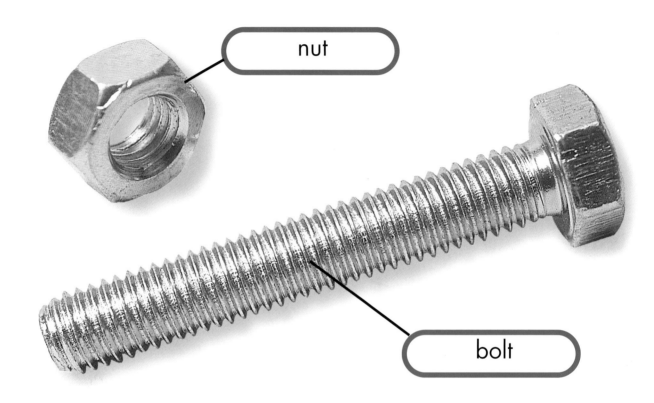

nut

bolt

Nuts and **bolts** always work together. A bolt has a **screw thread** on the outside. A nut has one on the inside. Turning a nut makes it move along a bolt.

bolt

We join things together with nuts and bolts. You put the bolt through holes in the objects and turn the nut with a **spanner**. This pulls the objects firmly together.

Screws for holding

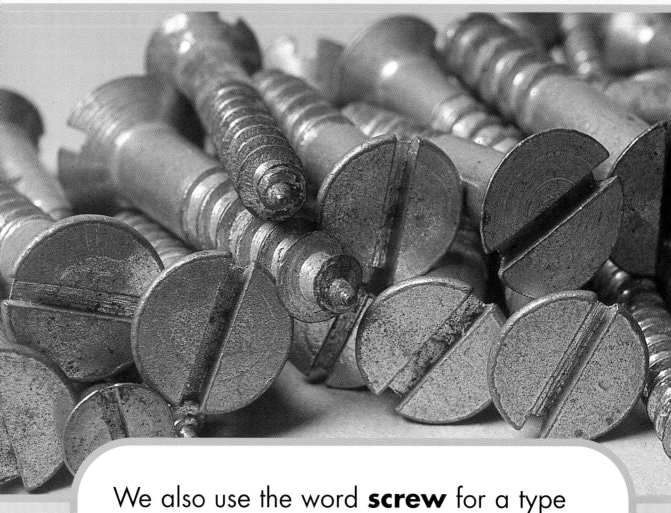

We also use the word **screw** for a type of metal fixing. A screw has a pointed end and a **screw thread**. These screws are for fixing things to wood.

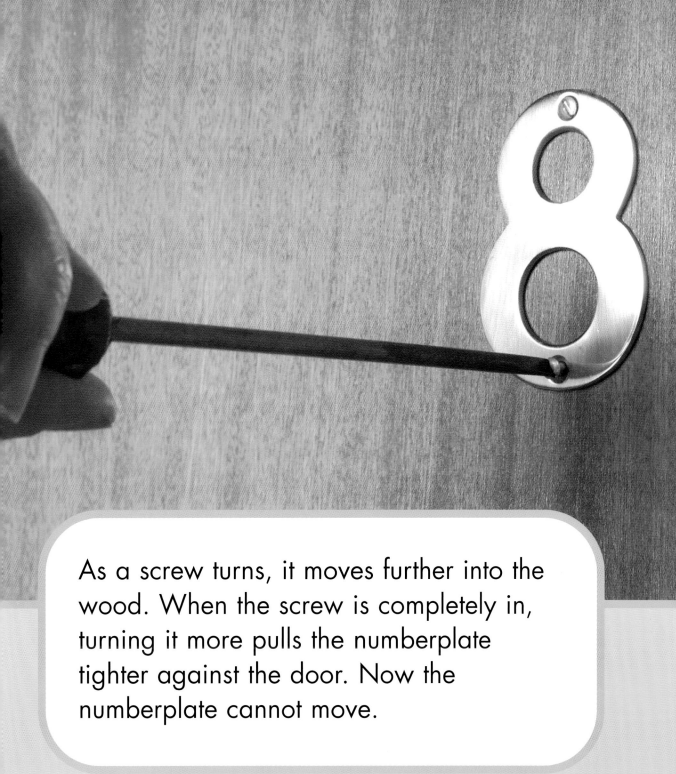

As a screw turns, it moves further into the wood. When the screw is completely in, turning it more pulls the numberplate tighter against the door. Now the numberplate cannot move.

Screws for drilling

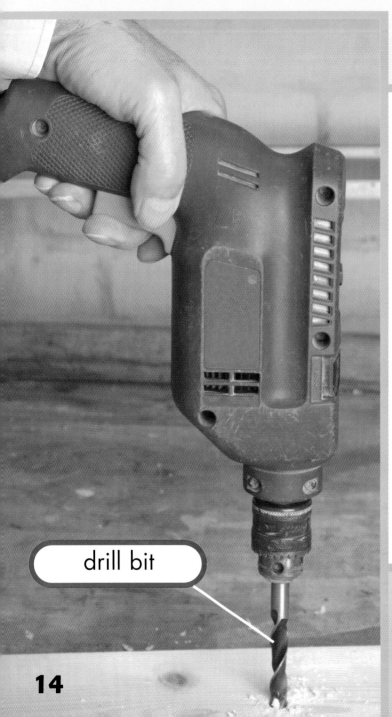

drill bit

We also use **screws** for drilling holes. The **drill bit** on this drill has a **screw thread**. The end cuts into the wood. The screw thread pushes the waste wood out of the hole it has made.

Here is another type of screw for drilling. An auger is like a giant drill bit. Fishermen use an auger to drill holes in the ice, so they can catch fish.

Screws for gripping

We also use **screws** for gripping things tightly. This **device** is called a clamp. Tightening the clamp makes the screw move until it holds the pieces of wood firmly together.

A vice is like a clamp. It holds an object still while you drill or cut it. Turning the handle makes screws pull the two sides of the vice together.

Screws for squashing

Turning a **screw** makes a big push. So screws are good for squashing things. This is a screw press. Turning the handle squashes the fruit inside to get the juice out.

Inside a plastic bottle top is a plastic **disc**. When the top is screwed on, it squashes the disc to make an **airtight seal**. This stops the drink going flat.

Screws for lifting

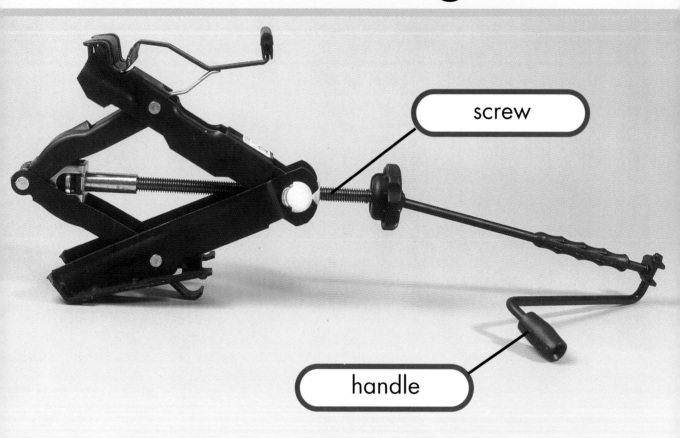

screw

handle

We use **screws** for lifting and supporting objects. A jack is a **device** for lifting a car. Across the middle is a very long screw with a handle on the end.

Turning the jack's handle pulls the two sides of the jack together. The jack pushes up on the car. The screw means that a small push on the handle lifts the heavy car.

Screws for moving

propeller

If we spin a screw round, it can make things move. A boat **propeller** is like a big screw. When it turns, it pushes water backwards, which pushes the boat forwards.

This electric fan has fan blades shaped like
a large **screw thread**. When the electric
motor turns the blades, they push air
forwards. The moving air cools the room.

Adjusting with screws

screw thread
under seat

Each turn of a **screw** only makes the screw move backwards or forwards a tiny bit. Turning the seat of this stool makes it move up or down slightly.

You have to **focus** a **microscope** to see the object clearly. The focus knob is a screw. Turning it slowly makes the microscope's tube move up or down just a tiny bit. This makes it easy to focus.

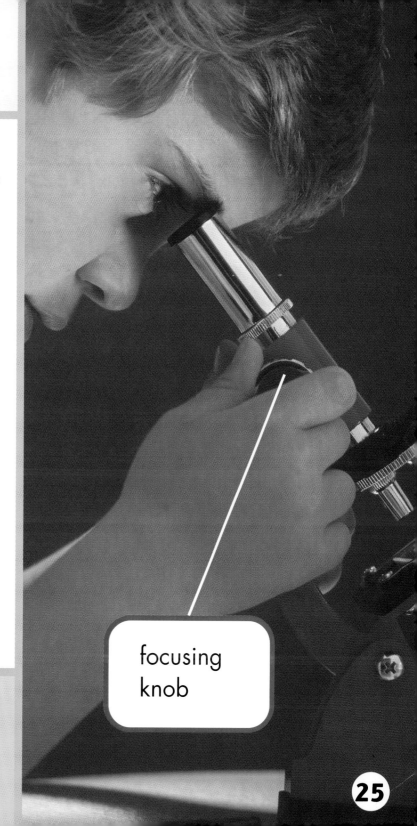

focusing knob

Screws in machines

screw

screw

Hundreds of complicated machines have **screws** inside that help them to work. Most machines, like this robot head, are held together by dozens of screws and **nuts** and **bolts**.

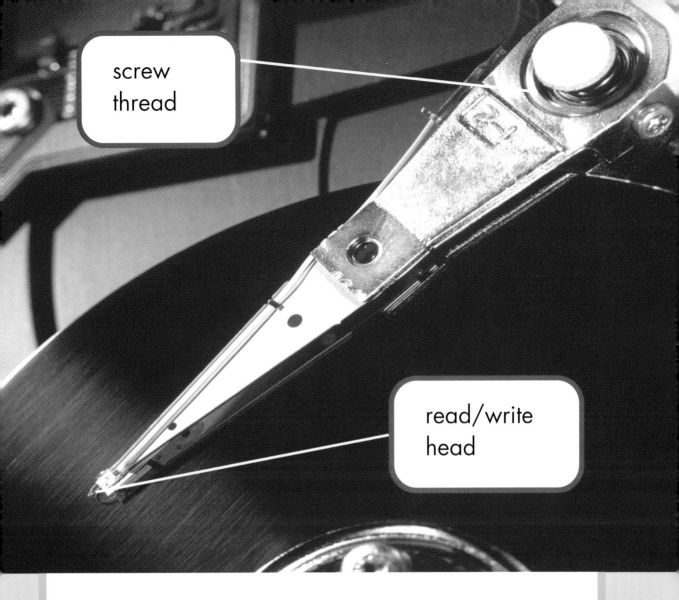

screw
thread

read/write
head

This is the inside of a computer's **disc drive**. The tiny **screw thread** moves the reading and writing **head** backwards and forwards across the disc.

Amazing screw facts

- The **screw** is one of the oldest machines in the world. It was invented in Greece more than 2000 years ago.
- An Archimedean screw is a long tube with a **screw thread** inside. In some places in the world it is used for lifting water from rivers onto fields.
- The first ship **propellers** were made nearly 200 years ago. They were called screws instead of propellers because they were shaped like huge screws.
- Scientists and **engineers** use screws for measuring things very accurately. They use a **device** called a micrometer screw gauge.

- Engineers use very big strong **nuts** and **bolts** to join the parts of a building frame together.

Glossary

airtight	stops air getting in or out
bolt	rod with a screw thread around the outside
device	thing that does a job. A clothes peg is a device. So is an electronic calculator.
disc	round, flat piece of material
disc drive	machine in a computer that stores information
drill bit	metal rod that fits into a drill and cuts a hole
engineer	person who designs, makes or mends machines
focus	to make an image sharp and clear
groove	long, very narrow hole
head	in a disc drive, part that reads or records data on to a disc

microscope	device that makes tiny objects look much bigger
motor	machine that turns power into movement
nut	square or hexagonal (six-sided) piece of material with a hole in the middle and a screw thread inside
propeller	object that pushes water or air when it spins round
screw	simple machine or a type of fixing with a screw thread around the outside and a sharp tip
screw thread	groove around the outside of a screw or bolt
seal	piece of material that stops water or air getting through a hole
spanner	tool for turning nuts or bolts

More books to read

What do Screws Do?, David Glover (Heinemann Library, 1996)

Screws, Angela Royston (Heinemann Library, 2000)

What is a Screw?, Lloyd G. Douglas (Children's Press, 2002)

What are Screws?, Helen Frost (Pebble Books, 2001)

Index

Titles in the *Very Useful Machines* series include:

Hardback   0 431 17892 5

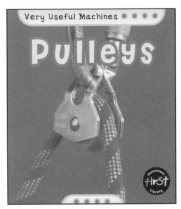

Hardback   0 431 17893 3

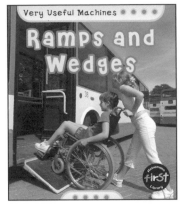

Hardback   0 431 17896 8

Hardback   0 431 17894 1

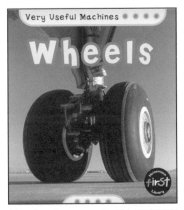

Hardback   0 431 17895 X

Find out about the other titles in this series on our website www.heinemann.co.uk/library